Let's C.E.O.

Cover Each Other and Lead with Legacy

By Cherisse Stephens

Let's C.E.O.

Cover Each Other and Lead with Legacy

By Cherisse Stephens

Published by Praisem Worldwide Publishing Company

International Standard Book Number

979-8-218-77019-8

FORWARD

There is a calling on your life to lead. Not simply to manage people or complete projects, but to impact lives, shift cultures, and leave a legacy that outlives you. I wrote this book for women and men ready to embrace leadership as more than a title, who understand that influence is a responsibility, and that how we lead matters as much as the results we produce.

Let's C.E.O. began as a phrase I used in conversations with leaders who felt alone in their journeys. It grew into a movement because I believe leadership is not a solo act but a shared commitment to Cover Each Other. We live in a world that rewards competition, yet I have seen firsthand the transformation that happens when we choose collaboration.

Whether you are stepping into your first leadership role or carrying decades of experience, this book is for you. It is a guide, a conversation, and a challenge to lead with intentionality, empathy, and vision. I hope that as you turn each page, you will be reminded that you are not alone, and that your leadership has the power to change the world around you.

Introduction

Leadership is a journey. Some seasons will stretch you beyond your comfort zone, while others will affirm that you are exactly where you are meant to be. Over the years, I have learned that leadership is not only about vision and execution; it is about the heart, the mindset, and the relationships that sustain you along the way.

This book is built on a groundbreaking framework for people to lead boldly, lift others, and leave a legacy of excellence. It is a call to lead differently, through collaboration instead of competition, through covering instead of comparison, and through excellence that endures long after titles fade.

You will find that each chapter blends real-life lessons, research-backed insights, and practical applications. Reflection questions will invite you to slow down and think deeply about your leadership approach.

'Leadership in Action' sections will give you concrete next steps to put into practice immediately. My stories, victories, and mistakes are shared not for perfection's sake but to remind you that leadership is lived, not just learned.

As you read, I encourage you to journal your thoughts, try the exercises, and share these principles with other leaders in your circle. Leadership is multiplied when it is shared. Together, we can create a culture where women and men cover each other, lift each other, and leave a legacy that endures.

Chapter One: Let's C.E.O.

Cover Each Other and Lead with Legacy

Leadership is not a solo act; it is a shared responsibility. "Let's C.E.O." is not just a catchy phrase; it is a movement, a mindset, and a mission to empower leaders to Cover Each Other.

In a world where comparison often stifles collaboration, this book is a bold declaration that we are stronger when we lift one another. Authentic leadership begins when we stop trying to compete and start learning to cover. To C.E.O. is to lead with intentionality, empathy, and vision. It is to recognize that influence is not about position but about impact. This chapter lays the foundation for leading from a place of collaboration, not self-interest. We are not waiting to be chosen; we are choosing to lead together.

Whether you are a seasoned leader or just starting your leadership journey, the principle of covering each other is timeless. Veteran leaders can pour wisdom, connections, and encouragement into emerging people.

Meanwhile, new leaders bring fresh energy, innovative thinking, and a willingness to challenge old patterns. When these two perspectives unite, the result is a powerful synergy that elevates everyone.

In practice, covering each other means stepping in when someone needs support, offering resources when someone lacks them, and celebrating others' wins as if they were your own. It is about building a culture where leaders see one another as allies rather than rivals. Imagine the impact if every leader committed to mentoring one person and championing their success. The ripple effect would transform teams, organizations, and entire industries.

This book will also challenge you to evaluate your leadership mindset. Are you unknowingly competing with those you should be collaborating with? Are you holding back wisdom or opportunities out of fear that someone might surpass you?

True legacy is built when you help others rise, even if it means they one day stand beside or ahead of you.

Reflection Questions

1. How have you seen competition get in the way of collaboration?

2. Who in your circle can you cover today with encouragement or support?

3. What does legacy mean to you as a leader?

C.E.O. Reflections

Use this spacce to write your thoughts, takeaways, or action steps from this chapter.

_____

_____

_____

_____

_____

_____

_____

_____

_____

_____

_____

_____

_____

_____

_____

C.E.O. Reflections

Use this spacce to write your thoughts, takeaways, or action steps from this chapter.

_____

_____

_____

_____

_____

_____

_____

_____

_____

_____

_____

_____

_____

_____

_____

_____

Author's Reflection:

When I first stepped into leadership, I thought it was about proving myself. Over time, I realized the most powerful leaders I knew were not trying to be the loudest; they were lifting others. One of the greatest compliments I ever received was from a woman who said, 'You did not just lead me, you covered me.' That's legacy.

Chapter Two: Lead In Love

Leadership is deeply relational. You can have strategy, vision, and charisma, but your leadership will eventually feel hollow if you do not lead in love. Love is not weak; it is one of the strongest forces in leadership. It empowers, corrects, and connects. To lead in love is to value people over performance.

It means showing up with compassion, practicing forgiveness, and making room for others to grow. Love is patient and persistent. It reminds us that people are not problems to fix; they are souls to shepherd. Scripture reminds us in Corinthians 1:13 that without love, we are nothing. Leading in love means listening well, serving first, and correcting with care. It transforms environments and cultivates trust. Whether you lead a team, a ministry, or a movement, love must be your foundation.

For the emerging leader, leading in love means understanding that people are more than their roles. For the seasoned leader, it is the reminder that the greatest influence comes from how you treat those you lead. Both perspectives are essential. The leader who achieves this balance leaves a legacy of trust, honor, and loyalty.

Practical Ways to Lead in Love:

1. Begin meetings with affirmations or gratitude.

2. Offer feedback that builds rather than breaks.

3. Create spaces for open dialogue and vulnerability.

4. Celebrate milestones, both personal and professional.

Reflection Questions:

1. In what ways do you show love in your leadership?

2. Have you ever experienced leadership that lacked love? How did it feel?

3. What would leading your current assignment with more love look like?

C.E.O. Reflections

Use this spacce to write your thoughts, takeaways, or action steps from this chapter.

_____

_____

_____

_____

_____

_____

_____

_____

_____

_____

_____

_____

_____

_____

_____

_____

_____

C.E.O. Reflections

Use this spacce to write your thoughts, takeaways, or action steps from this chapter.

_____

_____

_____

_____

_____

_____

_____

_____

_____

_____

_____

_____

_____

_____

_____

_____

_____

Author's Reflections:

Some of my most significant leadership breakthroughs did not come through strategy; they came through love. The moments I stopped to affirm someone's worth, listen deeply, and stay present in someone's struggle are those I remember. My legacy is not just in what I have accomplished, but in who I have covered, encouraged, and empowered.

Chapter Three: Mind Matters Leadership Begins in the Mind

The greatest leadership battles are often waged in the mind. How we think determines how we lead. A leader's mindset can either be a launchpad or a limitation. Scientific research supports that a leader's ability to self-regulate, focus on growth, and maintain emotional resilience is central to organizational success.

Every action we take as leaders begins with a thought. If our thoughts are rooted in fear, comparison, or inadequacy, our leadership reflects that. But if our thoughts are grounded in clarity, confidence, and vision, we lead with conviction and consistency.

For new leaders, cultivating a strong mindset means developing confidence in your unique voice and decision-making ability. For experienced leaders, it is about maintaining mental resilience in the face of complex challenges and pressures.

The mind is the birthplace of legacy, and when leaders prioritize their mental well-being, they become more effective and influential.

Practical Strategies for a Strong Leadership Mindset:

1. Start each day with affirmations that align with your leadership values.

2. Practice mindfulness to improve focus and reduce stress.

3. Seek mentorship or coaching for continued mental growth.

Positive thought patterns lead to better decision-making, more innovative thinking, and stronger team dynamics. Leaders who think expansively inspire others to do the same, creating a ripple effect of growth and empowerment.

Reflection Questions:

1. What thoughts do you need to reframe to lead more effectively?

2. Are there internal narratives keeping you from showing up fully?

3. How can you renew your mind daily to reflect the leader you are becoming?

C.E.O. Reflections

Use this spacce to write your thoughts, takeaways, or
action steps from this chapter.

_____

_____

_____

_____

_____

_____

_____

_____

_____

_____

_____

_____

_____

_____

_____

C.E.O. Reflections

Use this spacce to write your thoughts, takeaways, or
action steps from this chapter.

_____

_____

_____

_____

_____

_____

_____

_____

_____

_____

_____

_____

_____

_____

_____

_____

_____

Author's Reflections:

I remember a season when I doubted whether I was equipped to handle the opportunities in front of me. The thoughts I wrestled with were not about ability but identity. It took prayer, wise counsel, and consistent reflection to shift my mindset. Once I did, doors opened. My leadership flourished, not because my situation changed, but because I changed how I saw myself in it.

Chapter Four:

Collaboration Over Competition

Collaboration can feel countercultural in a culture that often glorifies individualism and competition. However, authentic leadership does not compete; it completes. When we choose to collaborate, we multiply our impact. Collaboration is a catalyst for innovation, unity, and growth.

For new leaders, collaboration can accelerate your development by giving you access to the wisdom, networks, and skills of others. For veteran leaders, it ensures your legacy extends beyond your achievements. Studies confirm that collaborative leadership drives creativity, increases job satisfaction, and improves overall team performance (Hoch & Kozlowski, 2014).

Collaboration invites us to move from scarcity to abundance, from protecting our turf to expanding the table. It means recognizing that someone else's win does not diminish your value. We all rise when we support each other's visions, celebrate each other's wins, and build platforms for others to stand on.

Reference:

Hoch, J. E., & Kozlowski, S. W. (2014). Leading virtual teams: Hierarchical leadership, structural supports, and shared team leadership. Journal of Applied Psychology, 99(3), 390–403.

Practical Ways to Foster Collaboration:

1. Host regular brainstorming sessions that invite ideas from every team member.

2. Partner with leaders in other industries to expand your reach and impact.

3. Share resources openly to create mutual growth opportunities.

4. Publicly recognize and celebrate the contributions of others.

One of the greatest lessons I have learned is that my light does not dim because I help someone else shine. I once helped a fellow leader organize an important event. I was not the keynote speaker; I was behind the scenes. The joy I felt watching her succeed reminded me that legacy is not built solely on the stage but in the hearts we lift.

Reflection Questions:

1. What are some ways you can intentionally collaborate with other leaders?

2. Have you ever felt the sting of comparison or competition? How did it affect you?

3. What does supporting someone else's vision look like for you this season?

C.E.O. Reflections

Use this spacce to write your thoughts, takeaways, or action steps from this chapter.

_____

_____

_____

_____

_____

_____

_____

_____

_____

_____

_____

_____

_____

_____

_____

_____

C.E.O. Reflections

Use this spacce to write your thoughts, takeaways, or action steps from this chapter.

_____

_____

_____

_____

_____

_____

_____

_____

_____

_____

_____

_____

_____

_____

_____

Author's Reflections:

As a leader, I have learned that collaboration is not just a tactic but a mindset. It requires humility to share the spotlight and wisdom to recognize that collective success far outweighs individual gain. My most meaningful leadership moments have come from being part of something bigger than myself.

Chapter Five: Leading with Emotional Wholeness

Leadership is often romanticized as boldness and strength, but authentic leadership is also rooted in emotional wholeness. Emotionally whole leaders are not perfect, but they are self-aware, grounded, and resilient. They lead from a place of healing, not hidden wounds.

Research shows that emotional intelligence is a major predictor of leadership effectiveness, team cohesion, and decision-making (Mayer, Salovey, & Caruso, 2021).

For emerging leaders, emotional wholeness begins with understanding your triggers and practicing healthy responses. For seasoned leaders, it means continuing to check your emotional health even when you have years of experience. The higher you go in leadership, the more your emotional state influences those you lead.

When leaders ignore their emotional health, it creates cracks in their influence. Unchecked anxiety, burnout, or insecurity can leak into our communication, decisions, and relationships. However, when we do the inner work, acknowledging our emotions, seeking healing, and setting boundaries, we lead with more clarity and compassion.

Reference:

Mayer, J. D., Salovey, P., & Caruso, D. R. (2021). Emotional intelligence: New ability or eclectic traits? American Psychologist, 76(3), 400–410.

Practical Strategies for Emotional Wholeness:

1. Schedule regular mental health check-ins with a mentor, counselor, or trusted peer.

2. Keep a journal to process your thoughts and identify emotional patterns.

3. Set clear boundaries to protect your time and energy.

4. Engage in activities that restore you, whether prayer, exercise, creative hobbies, or time in nature.

Being busy does not mean being productive. Leading from a place of constant depletion leads to burnout. Learning how to pause, rest, and reset emotionally is essential for sustainable leadership. It also means permitting ourselves to say "no" so we can say "yes" to what matters most.

Reflection Questions:

1. Are you leading from a place of wholeness or burnout?

2. What emotional habits support or hinder your leadership?

3. What does emotional rest look like for you?

C.E.O. Reflections

Use this spacce to write your thoughts, takeaways, or action steps from this chapter.

_____

_____

_____

_____

_____

_____

_____

_____

_____

_____

_____

_____

_____

_____

_____

_____

C.E.O. Reflections

Use this spacce to write your thoughts, takeaways, or action steps from this chapter.

_____

_____

_____

_____

_____

_____

_____

_____

_____

_____

_____

_____

_____

_____

_____

_____

_____

Author's Reflections:

There was a time when I was leading, serving, and speaking, but I was emotionally exhausted. I had taken on so many assignments that I did not realize I was pouring from an empty cup. What helped me most was a mentor who lovingly confronted me and encouraged me to change my thought process. It was not easy to hear, but eventually I embraced her wisdom.

Chapter Six: The Power of Disagreement

Disagreement does not have to be divisive. Some of the strongest leadership teams thrive because they have learned to navigate conflict respectfully and purposefully. Constructive disagreement sharpens ideas, challenges assumptions, and strengthens strategies. When handled well, disagreement becomes a tool for growth.

For leaders just starting, learning to handle disagreement early in your career will help you navigate future challenges with grace. For experienced leaders, refining your conflict resolution skills can deepen trust within your team and foster innovation. According to Stone and Heen (2014), leaders who welcome respectful dissent are likelier to cultivate innovation and psychological safety.

Leadership requires discernment in knowing when to listen, when to stand firm, and when to yield. Healthy disagreement invites dialogue and creates an environment where people feel safe to share differing opinions without fear of rejection.

Practical Strategies for Navigating   Disagreement:

1. Listen fully before forming your response.

2. Separate the issue from the individual, focus on ideas, not personalities.

3. Seek common ground and shared goals.

4. Keep the discussion anchored in mutual respect.

There was a season where I had to lead through a difficult time. A fellow leader challenged my thinking and offered a new perspective that, honestly, I resisted at first. I was convinced I was right, but her wisdom pushed me to see things differently. That moment not only shifted my perspective but also matured my leadership.

When rooted in honor and humility, disagreement can become a bridge to deeper understanding. It sharpens, humbles us, and grows our capacity to lead with courage and clarity.

Reference:

Stone, D., & Heen, S. (2014). *Thanks for the feedback: The science and art of receiving feedback well.* Viking.

Reflection Questions:

1. How do you typically respond to disagreement?

2. Have you experienced growth from a moment of healthy conflict?

3. What leadership practices can help you embrace respectful dissent?

C.E.O. Reflections

Use this spacce to write your thoughts, takeaways, or action steps from this chapter.

_____

_____

_____

_____

_____

_____

_____

_____

_____

_____

_____

_____

_____

_____

_____

C.E.O. Reflections

Use this spacce to write your thoughts, takeaways, or
action steps from this chapter.

_____

_____

_____

_____

_____

_____

_____

_____

_____

_____

_____

_____

_____

_____

_____

Author's Reflections:

I used to view disagreement as a threat to unity. However, I have learned that it is often the beginning of deeper collaboration. The key is staying rooted in humility and committed to resolution. One disagreement helped me become a better listener and a better leader.

Chapter Seven: The Power of Alignment

Alignment in leadership is about consistency between your words, actions, values, and vision. When leaders are aligned internally and externally, they operate with clarity and purpose. People follow not just because of charisma but because of congruence. They trust that what they see matches what they hear.

For leaders just beginning their journey, alignment ensures you do not compromise your core values in pursuing opportunity. For veteran leaders, it is a constant checkpoint to ensure that experience and influence are anchored in integrity. When alignment is strong, leaders inspire confidence, reduce organizational friction, and increase overall effectiveness.

When we are out of alignment, it shows. It may appear as burnout, confusion, or inconsistency in decision-making. However, when everything in us is working toward a unified direction, we lead more effectively and influence more deeply. Alignment is not about perfection; it is about integrity. When what you believe and what you build match, that is power.

Think of alignment like the wheels of a car. If one is out of balance, the whole ride feels off. In the same way, when one area of a leader's life is misaligned, whether it is relationships, responsibilities, or rest, it throws everything off course. Emotional, spiritual, and strategic alignment are all essential to sustainable leadership.

Practical Alignment Strategies:

1. Revisit your mission statement quarterly to ensure it reflects your current purpose.

2. Surround yourself with trusted advisors who will speak truth when you drift off course.

3. Keep your calendar aligned with your priorities; if it does not fit the vision, say no.

4. Integrate personal well-being into your leadership plan.

Aligned leaders create healthier organizational cultures and inspire more committed teams. If your values match your organization's or assignment's mission, you experience greater fulfillment and impact.

Leadership Alignment Self-Assessment:

On a scale from 1 (low) to 5 (high), rate yourself in these areas:

My daily actions reflect my stated values.

My leadership decisions align with my mission.

I regularly check in with mentors or accountability partners.

I feel energized rather than drained by my leadership role.

My personal life and professional life are in harmony.

C.E.O. Reflections

Use this spacce to write your thoughts, takeaways, or
action steps from this chapter.

_____

_____

_____

_____

_____

_____

_____

_____

_____

_____

_____

_____

_____

_____

_____

_____

_____

C.E.O. Reflections

Use this spacce to write your thoughts, takeaways, or action steps from this chapter.

_____

_____

_____

_____

_____

_____

_____

_____

_____

_____

_____

_____

_____

_____

_____

_____

Author's Reflections:

I remember seasons when I was frustrated by what had not happened yet, the things I thought should have come sooner. I chased opportunities that looked good but did not fit my actual assignment.

In time, I learned that God's timing is not ours. Waiting is not wasted; it is where patience makes room for new possibilities. When I slowed down and realigned with purpose, the shift was not instant but freeing. Now I lead with more peace, more clarity, and more joy.

Chapter Eight: Leading Beyond the Spotlight

Authentic leadership is not always about being in the spotlight. It is often found in the quiet decisions, the unseen sacrifices, and the moments when no applause follows. Leading beyond the spotlight means you are committed to impact, not attention. You understand that purpose is greater than popularity.

For leaders at the beginning of their journey, this chapter reminds them that every meaningful legacy is built in the hidden seasons. For seasoned leaders, it is a call to remember that visibility does not determine value. Many of the most transformational leaders throughout history have made their most significant contributions without the world ever knowing their names.

Many leaders are called to spaces without a platform, but their influence runs deep. It shows up in the people they mentor, the environments they shift, and the systems they build. Leading behind the scenes does not diminish your power; it refines it. You are shaping culture, even if the world does not see it immediately.

In a time when social media metrics and public recognition can be mistaken for leadership effectiveness, it is critical to return to the heart of servant leadership. Studies show that servant leadership, centered on humility, service, and authenticity, builds stronger, more resilient teams (Eva et al., 2019). Servant leaders prioritize the growth and well-being of their people above their visibility.

Reference:

Eva, N., Robin, M., Sendjaya, S., van Dierendonck, D., & Liden, R. C. (2019). Servant leadership: A systematic review and call for future research. The Leadership Quarterly, 30(1), 111–132.

Practical Ways to Lead Beyond the Spotlight:

1. Mentor someone privately without expectation of public acknowledgment.

2. Contribute ideas in meetings without attaching your name to them.

3. Support another leader's vision wholeheartedly.

4. Celebrate the wins of your team members more than your own.

Reflection Questions:

Are you seeking validation or making an impact?

How do you lead when no one is clapping?

What habits keep you grounded in purpose over popularity?

Leadership Growth Exercise:

For one week, identify at least one action you can take daily that benefits someone else's leadership without drawing attention to yourself. Document the experience and reflect on how it impacted your perspective.

C.E.O. Reflections

Use this spacce to write your thoughts, takeaways, or action steps from this chapter.

_____

_____

_____

_____

_____

_____

_____

_____

_____

_____

_____

_____

_____

_____

_____

_____

C.E.O. Reflections

Use this spacce to write your thoughts, takeaways, or
action steps from this chapter.

_____

_____

_____

_____

_____

_____

_____

_____

_____

_____

_____

_____

_____

_____

_____

Author's Reflections:

There were seasons when I led initiatives that no one saw. I showed up, prayed through, and poured out with no public affirmation. The fruit came later, in testimonies, in transformed lives, in the quiet confirmation from God that it mattered. I understand it is not about being seen. It is about being faithful.

I discovered a deeper strength in that faithfulness: that authentic leadership is forged in hidden places. The unseen sacrifices, the prayers whispered in silence, and the persistence to keep going when no one clapped, all became the training ground for greater impact. When the platform comes, I carry the lessons of success and the humility of knowing that God sees long before people do.

Chapter Nine: The Power of Rest

Leadership does not have to mean running on empty. We live in a culture that often equates productivity with worth, but rest is not weakness; it is wisdom. True leaders know how to pause, refuel, and protect the well-being of their mind, body, and spirit.

Rest is more than sleep. It is permission to disconnect from the demands of others so you can reconnect with the direction of God. It is choosing stillness without guilt and restoration without apology. When you rest well, you lead well.

For leaders just starting, the temptation may be to prove yourself through endless work constantly. For seasoned leaders, the challenge is often learning to step back from an unsustainable pace. Both must recognize that their greatest clarity, creativity, and compassion come from intentional rest.

Research continues to affirm the connection between rest and leadership performance. According to McEwen and Gianaros (2022), chronic stress impairs cognitive flexibility, emotional regulation, and decision-making, three essentials for effective leadership. When physically exhausted and emotionally depleted, we cannot lead with clarity.

Reference:

McEwen, B. S., & Gianaros, P. J. (2022). Central role of the brain in stress and adaptation: Links to socioeconomic status, health, and disease. Annals of the New York Academy of Sciences, 1506(1), 176–194.

Practical Rhythms of Rest for Leaders:

1. Schedule non-negotiable rest days into your calendar.

2. Create evening routines that prepare your mind and body for deep sleep.

3. Unplug from all devices for a set period each week.

Reflection Questions:

What does rest look like for you in this season?

Where have you glorified busyness over balance?

How can you build rhythms of rest into your leadership lifestyle?

Leadership Growth Exercise:

Block off one day this month where you intentionally rest without engaging in leadership responsibilities. Journal your mental, emotional, and spiritual state before and after.

C.E.O. Reflections

Use this spacce to write your thoughts, takeaways, or action steps from this chapter.

_____

_____

_____

_____

_____

_____

_____

_____

_____

_____

_____

_____

_____

_____

_____

_____

C.E.O. Reflections

Use this spacce to write your thoughts, takeaways, or action steps from this chapter.

_____

_____

_____

_____

_____

_____

_____

_____

_____

_____

_____

_____

_____

_____

_____

_____

Author's Reflections:

There was a time when I believed rest was for later. I pushed, poured, and persevered until I realized I was pouring from an empty vessel. My breakthrough came when I scheduled rest as a non-negotiable, not a reward. I discovered that my clarity, creativity, and confidence were
directly connected to how well I rested.

Chapter Ten: Legacy Leadership

Legacy is not what you leave behind but what you build daily. Legacy leadership is about leading with the future in mind, intentionally shaping what others will carry long after you have stepped away. It is not about fame but about fruit.

Leaders who think in terms of legacy are not easily distracted. They prioritize people over platforms and impact over image. They ask questions such as:
What will remain after I am gone? Who will continue the work I have started? What seeds am I sowing in this season?

For emerging leaders, this perspective can help shape early decisions to focus on building a strong foundation rather than chasing quick wins. For experienced leaders, it is a reminder that the systems, structures, and relationships you nurture now will echo for years.

According to Miller and Le Breton-Miller (2021), legacy-oriented leadership cultivates long-term thinking, ethical decision-making, and stronger organizational cultures. Leaders who mentor others, document vision, and build sustainable systems leave more than a memory; they leave a movement.

Reference:

Miller, D., & Le Breton-Miller, I. (2021). Family firm governance and legacy: A stewardship perspective. Journal of Family Business Strategy, 12(2), 100384.

Practical Ways to Build Legacy:

1. Invest in mentoring and developing the next generation of leaders.

2. Document your processes, values, and lessons learned.

3. Create sustainable structures that can function without your direct involvement.

4. Share both successes and challenges.

Reflection Questions:

What do you want to be remembered for as a leader?

Who are you mentoring or pouring into?

What systems or structures are you building that can last beyond you?

Leadership Growth Exercise:

Write a "Legacy Letter" to those you lead, outlining the values, principles, and vision you want to pass on. Please share it with a trusted group or keep it as a personal leadership compass.

C.E.O. REFLECTIONS
CHOOSING YOUR BOARD OF DIRECTORS:
A HEART-CHECK

Leadership isn't just about who sits at the table—it's about who you trust with your vision. Use these reflection questions to guide your thinking as you identify the right people for your Board of Directors.

1. Can I trust this person to speak the truth in love, even if it's uncomfortable?

   *My reflection:*_____

   _____

   _____

2. Has this person shown loyalty to the mission—not just to me personally?

   *My reflection:*_____

   _____

   _____

   _____

   _____

C.E.O. Reflections

Use this spacce to write your thoughts, takeaways, or action steps from this chapter.

_____

_____

_____

_____

_____

_____

_____

_____

_____

_____

_____

_____

_____

_____

_____

_____

C.E.O. Reflections

Use this spacce to write your thoughts, takeaways, or action steps from this chapter.

_____

_____

_____

_____

_____

_____

_____

_____

_____

_____

_____

_____

_____

_____

Author's Reflections:

I used to think legacy was about one significant, life-changing achievement. However, I have seen that legacy is built in the day-to-day, the consistent choices to show up, love well, and lead with humility and conviction. When I look at the women I have mentored, the organizations I have led, and the faith I have passed on, I know I am walking in the legacy every day.

The Call to Let's C.E.O.

Leadership is not just a title but a posture of the heart. Through every chapter of this book, you have been invited to reflect, realign, and rise as a leader who Covers Each Other and Leads with Legacy. The lessons shared here are more than strategies; they are soul-level principles that shape how you lead, live, and love.

Now, the journey is yours to continue.

Let's C.E.O. is not just a concept; it is a calling. It is a community of courageous women and men who are bold enough to lead, humble enough to grow, and committed enough to uplift others as they climb. When one of us rises, we all rise.

As you step forward into your leadership journey, whether you are just beginning or have been leading for decades, remember that your influence is not measured by achievements but by the lives you touch and the legacy you build. Leadership that covers, empowers, and inspires is leadership that lasts.

Let's C.E.O. - together.

Cover Each Other And Lead with Legacy

30 Power Points for Leaders

Chapter One – Let's C.E.O. - Cover Each Other and Lead with Legacy

1. Leadership is stronger when it is shared.

2. Covering others builds trust and multiplies influence.

3. Legacy grows when you lift others to stand beside or ahead of you.

C.E.O. Reflections

Use this spacce to write your thoughts, takeaways, or action steps from this chapter.

_____

_____

_____

_____

_____

_____

_____

_____

_____

_____

_____

_____

_____

_____

_____

_____

30 Power Points for Leaders

Chapter Two – Lead in Love

4. Love is a leader's most powerful strategy.

5. People are not projects; they are purpose.

6. Leadership without love will eventually lose loyalty.

C.E.O. Reflections

Use this spacce to write your thoughts, takeaways, or
action steps from this chapter.

_____

_____

_____

_____

_____

_____

_____

_____

_____

_____

_____

_____

_____

_____

_____

_____

30 Power Points for Leaders

Chapter Three – Mind Matters: Leadership Begins in the Mind

7. A leader's thoughts shape their results.

8. Replace self-doubt with self-discipline and vision.

9. Guard your mind; it is the birthplace of legacy.

C.E.O. Reflections

Use this spacce to write your thoughts, takeaways, or action steps from this chapter.

_____

_____

_____

_____

_____

_____

_____

_____

_____

_____

_____

_____

_____

_____

_____

_____

_____

30 Power Points for Leaders

Chapter Four – Collaboration Over Competition

10. Collaboration creates abundance; competition breeds scarcity.

11. Another leader's win does not diminish yours.

12. Collective success builds lasting impact.

C.E.O. Reflections

Use this spacce to write your thoughts, takeaways, or action steps from this chapter.

_____

_____

_____

_____

_____

_____

_____

_____

_____

_____

_____

_____

_____

_____

_____

30 Power Points for Leaders

Chapter Five – Leading with Emotional Wholeness

13. Wholeness fuels clarity, compassion, and confidence.

14. Unhealed leaders pass down unhealthy leadership.

15. Emotional rest is as vital as physical rest.

C.E.O. Reflections

Use this spacce to write your thoughts, takeaways, or action steps from this chapter.

_____

_____

_____

_____

_____

_____

_____

_____

_____

_____

_____

_____

_____

_____

_____

30 Power Points for Leaders

Chapter Six – The Power of Disagreement

16. Healthy disagreement sharpens vision and strategy.

17. Listen to understand, not just to reply.

18. Conflict handled with respect builds stronger teams.

C.E.O. Reflections

Use this spacce to write your thoughts, takeaways, or action steps from this chapter.

_____

_____

_____

_____

_____

_____

_____

_____

_____

_____

_____

_____

_____

_____

_____

30 Power Points for Leaders

Chapter Seven – The Power of Alignment

19. Alignment creates integrity between words and actions.

20. Leaders lose influence when purpose and practice do not match.

21. When values and vision agree, impact multiplies.

C.E.O. Reflections

Use this spacce to write your thoughts, takeaways, or action steps from this chapter.

_____

_____

_____

_____

_____

_____

_____

_____

_____

_____

_____

_____

_____

_____

_____

_____

30 Power Points for Leaders

Chapter Eight – Leading Beyond the Spotlight

22. True influence often happens off the stage.

23. Humility sustains leadership longer than popularity.

24. Service is the highest form of leadership.

C.E.O. Reflections

Use this spacce to write your thoughts, takeaways, or
action steps from this chapter.

_____

_____

_____

_____

_____

_____

_____

_____

_____

_____

_____

_____

_____

_____

_____

_____

30 Power Points for Leaders

Chapter Nine – The Power of Rest

25. Rest is not weakness; it is leadership wisdom.

26. Leaders who protect their well-being protect their legacy.

27. Stillness restores strength and creativity.

C.E.O. Reflections

Use this spacce to write your thoughts, takeaways, or action steps from this chapter.

_____

_____

_____

_____

_____

_____

_____

_____

_____

_____

_____

_____

_____

_____

_____

_____

30 Power Points for Leaders

Chapter Ten – Legacy Leadership

28. Legacy is built daily, not just in defining moments.

29. Some leaders sow seeds they may never see fully bloom.

30. Impact outlasts titles, positions, and platforms.

C.E.O. Reflections

Use this spacce to write your thoughts, takeaways, or action steps from this chapter.

_____

_____

_____

_____

_____

_____

_____

_____

_____

_____

_____

_____

_____

_____

_____

_____

About the Author: Cherisse Stephens

Cherisse Stephens is a visionary author, philanthropist, mentor, and recognized leader who believes that success comes from lifting others as we climb. As the founder of The Cherisse Stephens Foundation, Inc. and the legally trademarked organization God's Cover-Girls, Inc., she has dedicated her career to empowering women and girls through mentorship, education, and building self-esteem.

In "Let's C.E.O. Cover Each Other and Lead with Legacy," Cherisse shares her revolutionary framework that transforms traditional leadership paradigms. Drawing from her extensive experience leading God's Cover-Girls, Inc., she demonstrates how leaders can create meaningful impact by choosing collaboration over competition, fostering environments where everyone thrives.

Through The Cherisse Stephens Foundation, Inc., Cherisse has built a platform beyond traditional mentorship. God's Cover-Girls, Inc. is a living example of her core philosophy. When we cover each other and lead with legacy in mind, we create lasting change that extends far beyond individual achievements.

Cherisse's unique approach to leadership has made her a sought-after speaker and mentor, focusing on empowering leaders to understand that their most significant legacy is not what they achieve alone but what they accomplish by covering, supporting, and elevating others along the way.

"Let's C.E.O. Cover Each Other and Lead with Legacy" represents Cherisse's commitment to reshaping how we think about success, leadership, and the legacies we leave behind, backed by years of real-world impact through her foundation work.

To Book Cherisse Stephens, visit our website @ CherisseStephens.com

References

Eva, N., Robin, M., Sendjaya, S., van Dierendonck, D., & Liden, R. C. (2019). Servant leadership: A systematic review and call for future research. The Leadership Quarterly, 30(1), 111–132. https://doi.org/10.1016/j.leaqua.2018.07.004

Hoch, J. E., & Kozlowski, S. W. (2014). Leading virtual teams: Hierarchical leadership, structural supports, and shared team leadership. *Journal of Applied Psychology, 99*(3), 390–403. https://doi.org/10.1037/a0030264

Mayer, J. D., Salovey, P., & Caruso, D. R. (2021). Emotional intelligence: New ability or eclectic traits? *American Psychologist, 76*(3), 400–410. https://doi.org/10.1037/amp0000716

McEwen, B. S., & Gianaros, P. J. (2010). Central role of the brain in stress and adaptation: Links to socioeconomic status, health, and disease. Annals of the New York Academy of Sciences, 1186(1), 190–222. https://doi.org/10.1111/j.1749-6632.2009.05331.x

Miller, D., & Le Breton-Miller, I. (2021). Family firm governance and legacy: A stewardship perspective. *Academy of Management Perspectives, 35*(2), 234–247. https://doi.org/10.5465/amp.2017.0004

Stone, D., & Heen, S. (2014). Thanks for the Feedback: The science and art of receiving feedback well. Viking (Penguin).